Are Sleeping

A Lift-the-Flap Book of Time Around the World

Durga Bernhard

Charlesbridge

While you are reading,

10:00 PM
22:00
● Alaska

A F R I C A

on the other side of the world,

Nigeria

ATLANTIC
OCEAN

someone is getting dressed.

While you are carrying,

Nigeria
9:00 AM
09:00

ASIA

Japan

PACIFIC
OCEAN

someone is walking home with a friend.

While you are waving,

5:00 PM
17:00

Japan

NORTH AMERICA

Mexico

PACIFIC
OCEAN

someone is listening to sounds in the night.

2:00 AM
02:00

Mexico

While you are dozing,

ASIA

someone is singing to her baby brother.

India

INDIAN
OCEAN

While you are washing,

India
1:30 PM
13:30

ASIA

Thailand

someone is climbing a tree.

Thailand

3:00 PM
15:00

While you are picking,

ATLANTIC
OCEAN

Haiti

someone is sleeping in the soft night breeze.

SOUTH
AMERICA

While you are dreaming,

Haiti
3:00 AM
03:00

EUROPE

United
Kingdom

ATLANTIC
OCEAN

someone is milking a goat.

While you are pouring,

ATLANTIC
OCEAN

Brazil

someone is pushing a boat from shore.

SOUTH AMERICA

Brazil ●

5:00 AM
05:00

While you are watching the sun rise,

far away across oceans and continents,

NORTH AMERICA

Alaska
(United States)

someone is going to sleep.

PACIFIC OCEAN

APR 14 2011

ARCTIC OCEAN

NORTH AMERICA

PACIFIC OCEAN

ATLANTIC OCEAN

Alaska (United States)

Haiti

Mexico

Brazil

SOUTH AMERICA

ATLANTIC OCEAN

PACIFIC OCEAN

Our Earth is a spinning globe. As the Earth turns, different parts of the world move into and out of sunlight. When it's nighttime for you, it's daytime on the other side of the world.

People divide the world into twenty-four time zones that start at the prime meridian. Going west, travelers must set their watches back one hour for each time zone they cross. Going east, they must set their watches forward one hour for each zone.*

The United States uses a twelve-hour clock that counts twelve hours from midnight to noon (AM), and twelve hours from noon to midnight (PM). Most countries use a twenty-four-hour clock that counts from midnight to midnight, or 00:00 to 24:00.

* Travelers visiting India must set their watches 5½ hours ahead of the time at the prime meridian.